SAYINGS
of the
BUDDHA

translated by

VEN. S. DHAMMIKA

GRAHAM BRASH, SINGAPORE

© Ven. S.Dhammika,1993

First published in 1993 by
Graham Brash (Pte) Ltd
227 Rangoon Road
Singapore 0821

ISBN 9971-49-283-0

Typeset by Points PrePress (Pte) Ltd
Printed by Express Printers, Singapore

Other titles in the series:
Sayings of Confucius
Sayings of Gandhi

Contents

Introduction

Siddhattha Gotama was born into a patrician family in northern India in 563 BCE. At the age of 29 he renounced his life of luxury and became one of the many ascetics who wandered through the towns and forests of ancient India in quest of truth. After six years of sitting at the feet of various teachers and experimenting with self-mortification he had a profound realisation, after which he came to be known as The Buddha, The Awakened One. The Buddha taught that when we die we are reborn and that we can have neither peace nor lasting happiness until this process of being born and dying ceases and a state called Nirvana is attained. Craving and ignorance compel us to be reborn and so the whole of the Buddha's teachings are aimed at replacing craving with contentment and ignorance with understanding. Rejecting belief in God and denying the efficacy of rites and rituals, the Buddha proclaimed that our fate in this world and the next depends not on our beliefs, but on the quality of our thoughts, speech and actions. After his death in 483 BCE the community of monks and nuns that the Buddha founded, the Sangha, spread his teachings throughout India and eventually beyond its borders to the far reaches of Asia. In today's world with its unrestrained acquisitiveness on one hand and religious fundamentalism on the other the Buddha's message of contentment, moderation and mental peace has particular appeal. The texts collected in this book are mainly from the Pali Tipitaka, the oldest and most authentic record of the Buddha's teachings while a lesser number are from the ancient commentaries.

Life & Death

1. "Imagine that the whole earth was covered with water, and a man was to throw a yoke with a hole in it into the water. Blown by the wind, that yoke would drift north, south, east and west. Now, suppose that once in a hundred years a blind turtle would rise to the surface. What do you think? Would that turtle put his head through the hole in the yoke as he rose to the surface once in a hundred years?"

   "It is unlikely, Lord."

   "Well, it is just as unlikely that one will be born as a human being; it is just as unlikely that an Enlightened One, a Noble One, a fully enlightened Buddha should arise in the world; and it is just as unlikely that the Dhamma and discipline of the Enlightened One should be taught. But now you have been born as a human being, an Enlightened One has arisen and the Dhamma has been taught. Therefore, strive to realise the Four Noble Truths."

2. Many garlands can be made
   From a heap of flowers.
   Likewise, many good deeds can be done
   By one born human.

3. The Lord asked: "Which is greater? The little bit of

sand on my fingernail, or the great earth?"

"Lord, greater by far is the great earth. Tiny is the sand on your fingernail. The two cannot be compared." "So too, beings who are reborn as humans are few in number. Far greater are those who are reborn in non-human realms. Therefore, you should train yourself, thinking: "We will live earnestly."

4.   The wandering ascetic Sāmandakāni asked Venerable Sāriputta: "Pray, your Reverence, what is good and what is bad?"

"Your Reverence, rebirth is bad and the ceasing of rebirth is good. Where there is rebirth this bad may be seen: cold and heat, hunger and thirst, defecation and urination, contact with fire, rod and spear, even one's own relatives and friends abuse one when they congregate together. But when there is the ceasing of rebirth this good may be seen: no cold nor heat, no hunger and thirst, no defecation and urination, no contact with fire, rod and spear, and no abuse from one's relatives and friends when they congregate together."

5.   Life in the world is unpredictable and uncertain. Life is difficult, short and fraught with suffering.

Being born, one has to die; this is the nature of the world.
With old age there is death; this is the way things are.

When fruit is ripe, it may drop early in the morning.

In the same way, one who is born may die at any moment.

Just as all the pots made by all the potters
End in being broken,
So it is with the lives of all who are born.

Neither young nor old, foolish nor wise
Will escape the trap of death.
All move towards death.

They are overcome by death.
They pass on to another world.
A father cannot save his son nor a family its members.

Look! With relatives watching, with tears and crying,
Men are carried off one by one,
Like cattle to the slaughter.

So, death and ageing are a natural part of the world.
Thus, the wise grieve not, seeing the nature of the world.

6.   These five things should often be contemplated by both women and men, by both householder and home-leaver. What five? "Old age can come to me; I have not got beyond old age. Sickness can come to me; I have not got beyond sickness. Death can come to me; I have not got beyond death. I am the result of my own deeds, the heir to my deeds - deeds are the source, the kin and the foundation. Whatever deed I do, whether good or

bad, I shall become heir to that." These five things should often be contemplated by both women and men, by both householder and home-leaver.

7.   Mahānāma the Sakyan came to see the Lord, and said: "This town of Kapilavatthu is rich, prosperous, popular, crowded with men, thickly populated with people. Now, when I enter the city in the evening after waiting on the Lord or the monks, I meet with elephants, horses, chariots, carts and people, all swaying and rolling along. At such times, my thoughts that were fixed upon the Buddha, Dhamma and Sangha are utterly bewildered. Then I think: 'If I were to die at this moment, what would be my lot, where would I be reborn?' "

"Have no fear, Mahānāma, have no fear! Your death will be good, your end will be good. For one whose mind has for a long time been practised in faith, virtue, learning, in giving up and in wisdom, even though the body made of the four elements is devoured by birds and animals, yet the mind - if for a long time has been practised in faith, virtue, learning, in giving up and in wisdom - the mind soars aloft, the mind wins the highest. It is just as if a man were to plunge a jar of butter or oil into a deep pool of water and it were to be broken; the fragments of the jar would sink to the bottom but the butter or oil would float to the top. So Mahānāma, your mind has for a long time been practised in faith, virtue, learning, in giving up and in wisdom. So, have no fear. Your death will be good, your end will be good."

8.   Those who quarrel do not realise
       That one day we all must die.
       Those who do realise this
       Find little to quarrel about.

9.   In due time Kisā Gotami became pregnant, and after
ten lunar months gave birth to a son. But the child
died as soon as he was able to walk. Kisā Gotami had
not known death before, and when they came to remove
the child's body for cremation, she refused to let them
do so, saying to herself: "I will get medicine for my
son." Placing the dead child on her hip, she went from
house to house, asking: "Do you know a cure for my
son?" Everyone said to her: "Woman, you are
completely mad in seeking medicine for your son," but
she went away, thinking: "Truly, I will find someone
who knows the right medicine for my child." Now, a
certain wise man saw her and thought to himself: "I
must help her." So he said: "Woman, I do not know
if there is a cure for your child, but there is one who
will know, and I know him."
       "Sir, who is it who will know?"
       "Woman, the Lord will; go and ask him."
       So, she went to the Lord, paid reverence to him,
stood at one side, and asked: "Venerable sir, is it true
as men say that you know a cure for my child?"
       "Yes, I know."
       "What then do I need?"
       "A few mustard seeds."
       "I will get them, Venerable sir, but in whose house?"

"Get them from a house where no son or daughter or any other person has ever died."

"Very well, sir," Kisā Gotami said, and having paid reverence to the Lord, and having placed the dead child on her hip, she went to the village and stopped at the very first house.

"Have you any mustard seeds? They say that will cure my child." They gave her the seeds, and then she asked: "Friend, has any son or daughter died in this house?"

"What do you ask, woman? The living are few and the dead are many."

"Then take back your seeds, for they will not cure my child," she said, and gave back the seeds they had given her.

In this way, she went from house to house but never did she find one that had the mustard seeds that she needed, and she thought: "Oh! It is a difficult task that I have. I thought it was only I who had lost a child, but in every village the dead are more than the living." While she reflected, her heart which had quivered now became stable.

Speech

10. It is certain that a clod of earth
Thrown into the sky will fall to the ground;
So too the words of the supreme Buddha
Are always certain and reliable.

It is certain that the sun will rise
When the darkness of night fades away;
So too the words of the supreme Buddha
Are always certain and reliable.

It is certain that the lion will roar
As it emerges from its den;
So too the words of the supreme Buddha
Are always certain and reliable.

11. If a word has five marks it is well-spoken, not ill-spoken, not blameworthy nor condemned by the wise. It is spoken at the right time, it is spoken in truth, it is spoken gently, it is spoken about the goal and it is spoken with love.

12. Giving up lying, one becomes a speaker of the truth, reliable, trustworthy, dependable, not a deceiver of the

world. Giving up slander, one does not repeat there what is heard here, or repeat here what is heard there, for the purpose of causing divisions between people. Thus, one is a reconciler of those who are divided and a combiner of those already united, rejoicing in concord, delighting in concord, promoting concord; concord is the motive of his speech. Giving up harsh speech, one speaks what is blameless, pleasant to the ear, agreeable, going to the heart, urbane, pleasing and liked by all. Giving up useless chatter, one speaks at the right time, after the facts, to the point, about Dhamma and discipline, words worthy of being treasured, seasonable, reasoned, clearly defined and connected to the goal.

13.   Possessed of four qualities, one is understood as being a good person. What four?

Concerning this, the good person does not speak of what is to the discredit of another, even when asked. What then when asked? If, however, on being questioned, he is required to speak, then with reserve he dispraises the other person, with hesitation and in brief. This is the meaning of the saying: "This person is good."

Again, the good person, even when unasked, speaks of what is to the credit of another. What then when asked? If, however, on being questioned, he is required to speak, then without reserve he praises the other person, without hesitation and in full. This is the meaning of the saying: "This person is good."

Once again, the good person, even when unasked, speaks of what is to his own discredit. What then when asked? If, however, on being questioned, he is required to speak, then without reserve he speaks of what is to his own discredit, without hesitation and in full. This is the meaning of the saying: "This person is good."

Finally, the good person does not speak of what is to his own credit, even when asked. What then when asked? If, however, on being questioned, he is required to speak, then with reserve he speaks of what is to his own credit, with hesitation and in brief. This is the meaning of the saying: "This person is good."

14. The Lord said: "Words that have four qualities are well-spoken, not ill-spoken, faultless, not blamed by the wise. What four? Concerning this, one speaks words that are beautiful, not ugly; one speaks words that are right, not wrong; one speaks words that are kind, not cruel; one speaks words that are truthful, not false."

> The virtuous call beautiful speech the foremost,
> Secondly comes right speech, not wrong,
> Thirdly come kind words, not cruel,
> And fourthly comes truthful, not false speech.

Then Venerable Vangīsa moved from his seat, put his robe on one shoulder, joined his hands and said: "Something occurs to me, Lord." Then Venerable Vangīsa spoke these words in praise of the Lord:

One should utter only words
Which do no harm to oneself
Or cause harm to others;
That is truly beautiful speech.

Speak kind words,
Words rejoiced at and welcomed,
Words that bear ill-will towards no one;
And always speak kindly to others.

Truthful speech is of the Immortal.
This is an eternal law.
The virtuous stand firm on words
That are truthful, useful and right.

The Buddha speaks words that lead
To the winning of security,
The ending of sorrow and the attaining of Nirvāna.
Truly, this is the speech supreme.

15.   One whose mind is freed does not argue with anyone; he does not dispute with anyone. He makes use of the conventional terms of the world without clinging to them.

16.   "Good Gotama, for my part I say this, I hold this view. If anyone speaks of what he has seen, heard or sensed, there is no harm in him saying: This is what I saw, this is what I heard, this is what I sensed.' There is no harm resulting from that."

"For my part, Brāhmin, I do not say that everything one has seen, heard or sensed should be spoken of, and I do not say it should not be spoken of. If one speaks and unprofitable states grow, one should not speak. If one speaks and profitable states grow, one should speak of what one has seen, heard, sensed and understood."

17.   Potaliya, the wanderer, came to visit the Lord, greeted him courteously, and sat down at one side, and as he did, the Lord said to him: "Potaliya, there are these four persons found in the world. What four? Concerning this, one criticises that which deserves criticism at the right time, saying what is factual and true, but he does not praise that which deserves praise. Again, one speaks in praise of the praiseworthy at the right time, saying what is factual and true, but does not criticise that which deserves criticism. And again, one neither criticises that which deserves criticism, nor praises the praiseworthy. And finally, one criticises that which deserves criticism and praises the praiseworthy, at the right time, saying what is factual and true. Now of these four persons, which do you think is the most admirable and rare?"

"In my view, good Gotama, he who neither criticises that which deserves criticism nor praises the praiseworthy is the most admirable and rare. And why? Because his indifference is admirable."

"Well, I maintain that he who criticises that which deserves criticism and praises the praiseworthy, at the right time, saying what is factual and true - he is the best. And why? Because his timing is admirable."

18.   "If anyone should criticise me, the Dhamma or the Sangha, you should not on that account be angry, resentful or upset. For if you were, that would hinder you, and you would be unable to know whether they said right or wrong. Would you?"

"No, Lord."

"So, if others criticise me, the Dhamma or the Sangha, then simply explain what is incorrect, saying: 'That is incorrect, that is not right, that is not our way, we do not do that.' But also, if others should praise me, the Dhamma or the Sangha, you should not on that account be pleased, joyful or puffed up. For if you were, that would hinder you. So, if others praise me, the Dhamma or the Sangha, then simply explain what is correct, saying: 'That is correct, that is right, that is our way, that is what we do."

19.   The Lord approached the hermitage of the Brāhmin Rammaka where a large number of monks happened to be sitting, talking about Dhamma. The Lord stood outside the porch waiting for the talk to finish, and when it had, he coughed, knocked at the bar, and the monks opened the door. He sat down on the appointed seat and asked: "What were you talking about, monks? What was the talk that has just stopped?"

"We were talking about you, Lord."

"It is good for you who are young men from good

families, who have gone forth from home into homelessness, that when you meet together you speak either Dhamma or observe noble silence."

20.   Learn this from the waters:
In mountain clefts and chasms,
Loud gush the streamlets,
But great rivers flow silently.

Empty things make a noise,
The full is always quiet.
The fool is like a half-filled pot,
The wise man like a deep still pool.

21.   Again, it may be understood by a person's conversation whether or not he is competent at discussing things. If, on being questioned, a person is evasive, changes the subject, displays anger, malice or sulkiness, then he is incompetent to discuss things. If a person does not do these things, then he is competent at discussion.

Yet again, it may be understood by a person's conversation whether or not he is capable of constructive discussion. If, on being asked a question a person loads scorn on and beats down the questioner, laughs at him and tries to catch him out when he falters, then he is incapable of discussing things. If a person does none of these, then he is capable.

22.   Both now and in the past

It has always been thus, O Atula!

They blame those who are silent,
They blame those who speak much,
And they blame those who speak in moderation.
There is no one who is not blamed.

There never was,
There never will be
Nor is there now
A person who is wholly blamed or praised.

Generosity

23.   If beings knew as I know the results of sharing gifts, they would not enjoy their use without sharing them with others, nor would the taint of stinginess obsess the heart and stay there. Even if it were their last and final bit of food, they would not enjoy its use without sharing it, if there were anyone to receive it.

24.   "Is it possible, Lord, to see the visible results of generosity?"

And the Lord said: "Yes, it is possible to see the visible results of generosity. The giver, the generous one, is liked and dear to many. This is a visible result of generosity. The good and wise follow him. This is a visible result of generosity. A good reputation concerning him spreads about. This also is a visible result of generosity. Again, in whatever company he enters, be it nobles, Brahmins, householders or recluses, he enters with confidence and is untroubled. This is a visible result of giving. And finally, the giver, the generous one, after death is reborn in heaven. This is a result to be seen hereafter."

25.   The gift of truth excels all gifts.

26.   Vacchagotta said to the Lord: "I have heard it said that you, good Gotama, say that charity should only be given to you, not to others, to your followers, not to the followers of other teachers. Those who say this, are they representing your opinion without distorting it? Do they speak according to your teaching? For indeed, good Gotama, I am anxious not to misrepresent you."

The Lord said: "Vaccha, those who say this are not of my opinion, they misrepresent me by saying what is not true. Truly, whoever discourages another from giving charity hinders in three ways. What three? He hinders the giver from acquiring good, he hinders the receiver from getting the charity, and he has already ruined himself through his meanness."

27.   These five things make one's gift good. What five? One gives with reverence, one gives thoughtfully, one gives with his own hand, one gives things that are good, and one gives thinking of the result.

28.   There are these five timely gifts. What five? One gives to the one who has just arrived, to one who is leaving, to the sick, to the hungry, and the first fruits of field and orchard one gives to the virtuous.

29.   A believer can be recognised by three things. What three? He desires to see those who are virtuous; he desires to hear the good Dhamma; and with a heart free

from stinginess, he lives at home granting favours freely, and delighting in sharing things with others.

Virtue

30.   Unsurpassed is the Lord's way of teaching the Dhamma concerning one's proper conduct in virtue. One should be honest, faithful and without deception or chatter. One should refrain from hinting or belittling others, and should not always be looking to add to one's gain. One should keep one's sense-doors guarded and be moderate in appetite; a maker of peace, observant, active and strenuous in effort. One should not hanker after sensual pleasures but be a meditator, thoughtful and with proper conversation, steady-going, resolute and sensible. This is the unsurpassed teaching concerning a person's proper ethical conduct. This the Lord fully comprehends and beyond it nothing lies to be further comprehended. And in such matters there is no other recluse or Brāhmin who is greater or more enlightened than the Lord concerning ethical conduct.

31.   The good shine from afar
Like the Himalaya mountains.
The evil are unseen
Like an arrow shot into the night.

32.   What sort of Dhamma practice leads to great good for

oneself? Concerning this, the noble disciple reflects: "Here am I, fond of life, not wishing to die, fond of pleasure and averse to pain. If someone were to kill me I would not like it. Likewise, if I were to kill someone they would not like that. For what is unpleasant to me must be unpleasant to another and how could I burden someone with that?" As a result of such reflection one abstains from killing, encourages others to abstain from it and speaks in praise of such abstention.

Again, the noble disciple reflects: "If someone were to steal what was mine, I would not like it. Likewise, if I were to steal what belonged to someone else they would not like that. For what is unpleasant to me must be unpleasant to another and how could I burden someone with that?" As a result of such reflection one abstains from stealing, encourages others to abstain from it and speaks in praise of such abstention.

Again, the noble disciple reflects: "If someone were to have intercourse with my spouse I would not like it. Likewise, if I were to have intercourse with another's spouse they would not like that. For what is unpleasant to me must be unpleasant to another and how could I burden someone with that?" As a result of such reflection one abstains from wrong sensual desire, encourages others to abstain from it and speaks in praise of such abstention.

Once again, the noble disciple reflects: "If someone were to ruin my benefit by lying I would not like it. Likewise, if I were to ruin someone else's benefit by lying they would not like that. For what is unpleasant to me must be unpleasant to another and how could I burden someone with that?" As a result of such reflection one abstains from lying, encourages others to abstain from it and speaks in praise of such abstention.

A noble disciple reflects further: "If someone were to estrange me from my friends by slander, speak harshly to me or distract me with pointless, frivolous chatter I would not like it. Likewise, if I were to do this to another they would not like that. For what is unpleasant to me must be unpleasant to another and how could I burden another with that?" As a result of such reflection one abstains from slander, harsh speech and pointless chatter, encourages others to abstain from it and speaks in praise of such abstention.

33.   Do not think lightly of evil, saying:
"It will not come to me."
A drop at a time is the water pot filled.
Likewise, little by little
The fool is filled with evil.

Do not think lightly of good, saying:
"It will not come to me."
A drop at a time is the water pot filled.
Likewise, little by little
The wise one is filled with good.

34.   And how is cleaning of the body threefold? Concerning this, one abandons killing, lays aside the rod and the knife; one lives gently, kindly and feeling

compassion towards every living being. One abandons stealing the property of another, whether in the jungle or the village; things not given, one does not steal. One abandons sexual misconduct. One has no intercourse with girls under the guardianship of mother, father, brother, sister or relatives, with girls lawfully protected, already pledged to a husband, those undergoing punishment or those dressed with flowers and pledged to be married.

35.   Whoever, whether at morning, noon or night, practises righteousness of body, speech and mind - will have a happy morning, a happy noon and a happy night.

36.   Here in the world
One should train carefully in virtue,
For virtue when cultivated
Brings success near at hand.

The careful one should guard virtue,
Desiring the three types of happiness -
The praise of others, wealth,
And heaven after death.

Virtue is the foundation, the forerunner,
The origin of all that is good and beautiful,
And therefore one should purify one's virtue.

Virtue is the control, the restraint

And the delighting of the mind,
And thus the place where all Buddhas cross over,
Therefore, one should purify one's virtue.

37.   The fool may be known by his deeds; the wise one may be known by his deeds. Wisdom is illuminated by one's deeds.

38.
The doer of good rejoices here, rejoices there,
Rejoices both here and there.
He rejoices and is glad
As he recollects his own good deeds.

The doer of good delights here, delights there,
Delights both here and there.
The thought: "Good I have done"
Fills him with delight.
He delights all the more
When he goes to the realm of bliss.

39.   One who is virtuous, possessed of virtue, is like an antidote for destroying the poison of defilements in beings; he is like a healing balm for allaying the sickness of defilements in beings; he is like precious gems for giving beings all they wish; he is like a ship for beings to go beyond the four floods; he is like a caravan leader for taking beings across the desert of births; he is like the wind for extinguishing the three fierce fires in beings; he is like a great rain cloud for filling beings with good thoughts; he is like a teacher for making

beings train themselves in what is skilled; he is like a good guide for pointing out to beings the path to security.

40.   The king asked: "Venerable Nāgasena, which is greater, good or bad?"

"Good is greater, Sire; bad is only small."

"In what way?"

"Sire, someone, acting badly is remorseful, saying: 'An evil deed was done by me,' and thus evil does not increase. But someone doing good is not remorseful. Because of freedom from remorse, gladness arises, from gladness comes joy, because of joy the body is tranquil, with a tranquil body one is happy, and the mind of one who is happy is concentrated. One who is concentrated sees things as they really are, and in this way good increases."

41.   Abandon wrong. It can be done. If it were impossible to do, I would not urge you to do so. But since it can be done, I say to you: "Abandon wrong." If abandoning wrong brought loss and sorrow, I would not urge you to do so. But since it conduces to benefit and happiness, I urge you: "Abandon wrong." Cultivate the good. It can be done. If it were impossible to do, I would not urge you to do so. But since it can be done, I say to you: "Cultivate the good." If cultivating the good brought loss and sorrow, I would not urge you to do so. But since it conduces to benefit and happiness, I urge you: "Cultivate the good."

42.   For one who is virtuous, in full possession of virtue, there is no need for the purposeful thought: "May I be free from remorse." Because it is natural for one who is virtuous to be free from remorse. And for one free from remorse there is no need for the purposeful thought: "May I be joyful." Because it is natural for one who is free from remorse to be joyful.

43.   It is better to live one day
Virtuous and meditative,
Than a hundred years
Immoral and uncontrolled.

44.   Do not be afraid of doing good deeds. It is another name for happiness. I know well that good deeds lead to a ripening, and a blossoming, which brings pleasure, joy and happiness for a long time.

45.   These five advantages come to the virtuous man because of his practice of virtue. What five? Concerning this, the virtuous man, possessed of virtue, by reason of his earnestness, comes by great wealth. The virtuous man, possessed of virtue, gains a good reputation. Again, the virtuous man, possessed of virtue - into whatever company he enters, whether nobles, Brāhmins, householders or recluses - he does so confidently and unconfused. And again, the virtuous man, possessed of virtue, dies without bewilderment.

And lastly, the virtuous man, possessed of virtue, after death is reborn in heaven.

46.   Wisdom is purified by virtue, and virtue is purified by wisdom. Where one is, so is the other. The virtuous person has wisdom, and the wise person has virtue. The combination of virtue and wisdom is called the highest thing in the world.

Worldly Success

47.   There are these five disadvantages of wealth. What five? Wealth is in danger of fire, flood, kings, robbers and unloved heirs. Then, there are these five advantages of wealth. What five? With the help of wealth one can make oneself happy, one's parents happy, one's wife, children, servants, and workers happy, and one's friends and companions happy. And to recluses and Brāhmins one can make offerings with lofty aim, connected with a happy future, resulting in happiness, leading to heaven.

48.   Of little importance is the loss of such things as wealth. But a terrible thing it is to lose wisdom. Of little importance is the gaining of such things as wealth. Great is the importance of gaining wisdom.

49.   Ugga, the king's chief minister, said to the Lord: "Lord, it is amazing and astonishing how rich, wealthy and opulent Migarā Rohaneyya is!"

"What then, Ugga, is the amount of his treasure?"

"He has a million in gold; and of silver, who can say?"

"But is that a real treasure? Not that I say it is not,

but that is a treasure that is subject to fire, water, kings, robbers, enemies and unwanted heirs. But there are seven treasures that are not subject to such things. What seven? The treasures of faith, virtue, conscientiousness, fear of blame, learning, generosity and wisdom. These seven are not subject to fire, water, kings, robbers, enemies and unwanted heirs.

50.   Four things lead to worldly progress: achievement in alertness, in caution, in good friendship and achievement in balanced livelihood. And what is achievement in alertness? Concerning this, in whatever way one earns a living, whether by farming, trading, cattle rearing, archery, service to the king or by some craft, in that one becomes deft and tireless, gifted with an inquiring turn of mind into ways and means, and able to arrange and carry out the job.

And what is achievement in caution? Concerning this, whatever one earns by work and effort, collected by strength of arm and sweat of brow in a just and lawful manner, one husbands, watches and guards so that kings do not seize it, thieves do not steal it, fire or water do not destroy it, and unwanted heirs do not remove it.

And what is good friendship? Concerning this, in whatever village or town one lives, one associates with, converses with, discusses things with people either young or old, who are cultured, full of faith, full of virtue, full of charity and full of wisdom. One acts in accordance with the faith of the faithful, the virtue of the virtuous, the charity of the charitable and the wisdom of the wise.

And what is balanced livelihood? Concerning this, one knows both his income and expenditure and lives neither extravagantly nor in a miserly way, knowing that income after expenditure will stand at so much and that expenses will not exceed income. Just as a goldsmith or his apprentice knows, on holding the scales, that so much has dipped down and so much has tilted up, one knows income and expenditure. If one with a small income were to lead an extravagant life there would be those who would say: "He enjoys his wealth like a wood-apple eater." Likewise, if one with a good income were to be miserly, there would be those who would say: "He will die like a beggar." There are four channels through which the wealth one has collected is lost: debauchery, drunkenness, gambling and friendship with evil-doers. Imagine there was a great tank of water with four inlets and outlets, and a man was to close the inlets but keep the outlets open. If there was no rain we could expect the water to decrease. In the same way, these are the four channels through which wealth is lost. There are these four channels through which the wealth one has collected is preserved: avoidance of debauchery, drunkenness, gambling and friendship with evil-doers. Imagine there was a great tank of water with four inlets and outlets, and a man was to keep the inlets open and close the outlets. If he did this and there was good rainfall, we could expect the water to increase. In the same way, there are these four channels through which wealth is preserved.

51.　　　These five trades ought not to be practised by a

layman. What five? Trade in weapons, trade in human beings, trade in flesh, trade in alcohol and trade in poisons.

52.   There are these six dangers associated with idleness. Thinking: "It's too cold," one does not work. Thinking: "It's too hot," one does not work. Thinking: "It's too early," one does not work. Thinking: "It's too late," one does not work. Thinking: "I am too hungry," one does not work. Thinking: "I am too full," one does not work.

53.   With four things women win power in this world; this world is within their grasp. What four? Concerning this, a woman is capable at her work, she manages the servants properly, she is loved by her husband and she guards his wealth.

And how is a woman capable at her work? Whatever her husband's home employs, whether in wool or cotton, she is deft and tireless, gifted with an inquiring turn of mind into ways and means and able to arrange and carry out the job.

And how does she manage the servants properly? Whether there be servants, messengers or workers in her husband's household, she knows the work of each and what has been done, she knows what has not been done, she knows the strengths and weaknesses of the sick, and she divides the food, both hard and soft, according to their share.

And how is she loved by her husband? Whatever her

husband considers unlovely, she would never do, not even to save her life.

And how does she guard her husband's wealth? Whatever money, grain, silver or gold he brings home, she secures, watches and guards; never does she steal, misuse or waste it.

Friends and Friendship

54.   One who is wise and disciplined,
Kindly always and intelligent,
Humble and free from pride -
One like this will win respect.

Rising early and scorning laziness,
Remaining calm in times of strife,
Faultless in conduct and clever in actions -
One like this will win respect.

Being able to make friends and keep them,
Welcoming others and sharing with them,
A guide, philosopher and friend -
One like this will win respect.

Being generous and kindly in speech,
Doing a good turn for another
And treating all alike -
One like this will win respect.

55.   Cultivate a friend whose ways are seven. What seven? He gives what is hard to give, does what is hard to do, bears what is hard to bear, he confesses his own secrets and keeps your secrets, in times of trouble he does not

forsake you, and he does not forsake you when you are down.

56.   One who is clever should make no friends
                Among the malicious, the angry, the envious
                Or those who delight in the misfortunes of others.
                Truly, contact with the bad is evil.

                One who is clever should make friends
                Among those with faith, the pleasant, the wise,
                And those with great learning.
                Truly, contact with the good is blessed.

57.   Should you find a person who points out your faults
                As if indicating a hidden treasure
                Follow that wise and sagacious person.
                It will result always in good.
                Never in evil.

                Let him admonish you, instruct you
                And shield you from evil.
                He will be disliked by the worldly.
                But loved by the good.

58.   Who is one's own best friend, and who is one's own worst enemy? Those whose thoughts, speech and actions are evil, they are their own worst enemy. Even if they were to say: "We care about ourselves," nevertheless they would be their own worst enemy. And

why? Because that which one would do to an enemy, they do to themselves. Those whose thoughts, speech and actions are good, they are their own best friends. Even if they were to say: "We don't care about ourselves," nevertheless they would be their own best friend. And why? Because that which one would do to a friend they do to themselves.

59.   There are four types of people who should be known as enemies disguised as friends: the greedy person, one who speaks but does not act, the flatterer and the squanderer. The greedy person is an enemy disguised as a friend for four reasons. He is greedy; he gives little and asks much; if he does what he should, it is only out of fear, and he pursues his own interests only. He who speaks but does not act is an enemy disguised as a friend for four reasons. He reminds you of the good done on your behalf in the past; he talks of the good he will do on your behalf in the future; he tries to win your favour with empty words; when the opportunity to help arises, he pleads helplessness. The flatterer is an enemy disguised as a friend for four reasons. He encourages you to do wrong; he discourages you from doing right; he praises you to your face and speaks ill of you behind your back. The squanderer is an enemy disguised as a friend for four reasons also. He is your companion when you drink, when you frequent the streets at untimely hours, when you haunt low shows and fairs, and he is your companion when you gamble.

A friend who always wants to take,
A friend who says but doesn't do,
A friend who uses flattering words,
A friend who joins you in wrong -

These four friends are really foes,
And one who is wise, having understood this,
Will avoid them from afar,
As if they were a dangerous road.

There are four kinds of stout-hearted people who should be known as true friends: the helper, the friend in both good times and bad, one who gives good counsel, and one who sympathises. The helper is a true friend for four reasons. He guards you when you are off your guard; he guards your property when you are off your guard; he comforts you when you are afraid; and when something has to be done, he gives you twice what you require. The friend in both good times and bad is a true friend for four reasons. He tells you his secrets; he keeps the secrets you tell him; in trouble he does not forsake you; he would even lay down his life for you. The friend who gives good counsel is a true friend for four reasons. He discourages you from doing wrong, he encourages you to do good, he tells you things you have not heard, and he points out the way to heaven. The friend who sympathises is a true friend for four reasons. He is sad at your misfortunes, he rejoices at your good fortune, he restrains others from speaking ill of you, and he commends those who speak well of you.

A friend who always lends a hand,
A friend in both sorrow and joy,
A friend who offers good counsel,
A friend who sympathises too -

These are the four kinds of true friends,
And one who is wise, having understood this,
Will always cherish and serve such friends,
Just as a mother tends her only child.

60.   What is friendship with the good? It is to follow after, to frequent the company of and associate with people who are believers, virtuous, learned, generous and wise; to resort to and consort with them, to be devoted to them, enthusiastic about them, in unity with them.

61.   Then Ānanda came to the Lord and said: "Half of the holy life is friendship, association and intimacy with the beautiful."

"Say not so, Ānanda, say not so! It is the whole of the holy life, not half, this friendship, this association, this intimacy with the beautiful."

62.   If the one who does no wrong
Follows one who is evil,
He himself will be suspected of evil
And his reputation will decline.

According to the friends one makes,
According to who one follows,
So does one become.
Like one's associates one becomes.

Followed and followers,
Toucher and touched alike,
An arrow smeared with poison
Infects those arrows that are not poisoned,
So that all are fouled.
The upright person not wishing to be soiled
Should not keep company with the fool.

If one strings a piece of putrid fish
On a blade of kusa grass,
The grass will smell putrid too;
The same with one who follows the fool.

If one wraps frankincense
In an ordinary kind of leaf,
The leaf will soon smell sweet too;
The same with one who follows the wise.

Remembering the example of the leaf wrapping
And understanding the results,
One should seek companionship with the wise,
Never with the fool.

Oneself and Others

63.   One who wants to admonish another should first investigate: "Am I or am I not one who practises utter purity in body and speech? Am I or am I not possessed of utter purity in body and speech, flawless and untainted? Are these qualities manifest in me or not?" If they are not, there are undoubtedly people who will say: "Come now, practise correct bodily and verbal conduct yourself." There are people who would say this. Again, one who wants to admonish another should first investigate: "Have I developed a mind of goodwill, free from malice towards my fellows in the holy life? Is this quality established in me or not?" If one has not, there are undoubtedly people who will say: "Come now, develop a mind of goodwill yourself." There are people who would say this.

64.   There are these four types of persons found in the world. What four? He who is concerned neither with his own good nor the good of others, he who is concerned with the good of others but not his own, he who is concerned with his own good but not the good of others, and he who is concerned with both his own good and the good of others.

Just as a stick from a funeral pyre, burning at both ends and smeared with dung in the middle, can serve no useful purpose as fuel in the village or as timber in the forest - using such a simile do I speak of the person who is concerned neither with his own good nor the good of others. The person who is concerned with the good of others but not his own is more excellent and higher than this. The person who is concerned with his own good but not the good of others is more excellent and higher still. And he who is concerned with both his own good and the good of others - he is of these four persons the chief, the best, the topmost, the highest, the supreme.

Just as from a cow comes milk, from milk cream, from cream butter, from butter ghee, and from ghee the skimmings of ghee, and that is said to be the best - even so, the person who is concerned with his own good and the good of others is of these four persons the chief, the best, the topmost, the highest, the supreme.

65.   Once, the Lord dwelt among the Sakyas in the Park of the Banyan Tree at Kapilavatthu, and while there, Mahānāma the Sakyan came to him and asked: "How, Lord, does one become a lay disciple?"

"When one has taken refuge in the Buddha, the Dhamma and the Sangha, then one is a lay disciple."

"How, Lord, is a lay disciple virtuous?"

"When a lay disciple abstains from killing, stealing, sexual misconduct, lying and drinking intoxicants, then he is virtuous."

"How, Lord, does one help oneself but not others?"
"When one has achieved faith, virtue and renunciation, when one longs to see the monks, to hear the good Dhamma, to be mindful of the Dhamma once heard, when one reflects on it, knows it in both the letter and the spirit and walks in conformity with it, but one does not strive to establish such things in others, then one helps oneself but not others."

"How, Lord, does one help oneself and others?"

"When one has oneself achieved faith, virtue and renunciation and strives to establish such things in others, when one longs to see the monks, to hear the good Dhamma, to be mindful of the Dhamma once heard, when one reflects upon its meaning, knows it in both the letter and the spirit and walks in conformity with it and strives to establish such things in others, then one helps oneself and others too."

66.
Look not to the faults of others,
But rather look to your own acts,
To what you have done and left undone.

When one looks down on another's faults,
And is always full of envy,
One's defilements continually grow;
Far is one from their destruction.

If only you would do what you teach others,
Then, being yourself controlled,
You could control others well.
Truly, self-control is difficult.

You yourself must watch yourself.
You yourself must examine yourself,
And so, self-guarded and mindful,
O monk, you will live in happiness.

67.   One may not be skilled in the habit of other's thoughts but at least one can make this resolve: "I will be skilled in the habit of my own thoughts." This is how you should train yourself, and this is how it is done. A woman, a man or a youth fond of self-adornment, examining his reflection in a bright, clear mirror or a bowl of clear water might see a blemish or pimple and try to remove it. And when he no longer sees it there, he is pleased and satisfied and thinks: "It is an advantage to be clean." In the same way, one's introspection is most fruitful in good states when one thinks: "Am I usually greedy or hateful, overcome by sloth and torpor, with excited mind filled with doubt or anger, or am I not? Do I usually live with soiled thoughts, or clean thoughts? With body passionate or not, sluggish or full of energy, uncontrolled or well controlled?" If on self-examination one finds that he does live with these evil unprofitable states, then he must put forth extra desire, effort, endeavour, exertion, energy, awareness and attention to abandon them. And if on self-examination he finds that he does not live with the evil unprofitable states, then he should make an effort to establish those profitable states and further destroy the defilements.

68.   It is good from time to time to review one's own

faults; it is good from time to time to review another's faults. It is good from time to time to review one's own attainments; it is good from time to time to review another's attainments.

69.   Imagine a pool of turbid, stirred up and muddied water. Then, a man with vision might stand upon the bank. He could not see the oysters, the shells, the pebbles and gravel on the bottom or the fish moving about. And why? Because of the turbid state of the water. In the same way, it is impossible for one with a turbid mind to understand either his own benefit or the benefit of others, or to realise higher states. And why? Because of the turbid state of his mind. Now, imagine a pool of clear, tranquil and unstirred water. A man with vision might stand on the bank. He could see the oysters, the shells, the pebbles and gravel on the bottom, and the fish that move about. And why? Because of the untroubled state of the water. In the same way, it is possible for one with a tranquil mind to understand his own benefit and the benefit of others, and to realise higher states. And why? Because of the untroubled state of his mind.

70.   It is not possible that one who is himself unrestrained, undisciplined and unquenched could restrain, discipline and quench others. But it is very possible that one who is himself restrained, disciplined and quenched could make others like that also.

71.   All tremble at violence. All fear death.
        Put yourself in the place of others
        And kill no one nor have them killed.

72.   In this way one should draw this inference for
        oneself: "That person who has evil desires and is in the
        grip of evil desires - he is unpleasant and disagreeable
        to me. Similarly, if I were of evil desires and in the grip
        of evil desires, I would be unpleasant and disagreeable
        to others." When you see this, you should make up
        your mind to have no evil desires.

73.   A tree makes no distinction in the shade it gives.
        Even so, the meditator, the earnest student of
        meditation must make no distinction between any
        beings, but must develop love quite equally towards
        thieves, murderers, enemies and towards himself,
        thinking: "How may these beings be without enmity
        and without harm, how may they be at peace, secure
        and happy; how may they look after themselves?"

74.   At that time, the Lord said to the monks: "Once upon
        a time, a bamboo acrobat set up his pole, called his
        pupil, and said: 'Now, my lad, climb the pole and stand
        on my shoulders.' 'Alright, Master,' said the pupil, and
        he did what he was told. Then the master said: 'Now,
        my lad, you protect me and I will protect you, and
        protected and watched by each other we will do our act,

get a good fee, and come down safe and sound from the bamboo pole.' But then, the pupil said: 'No, no, Master! That will not do. You look after yourself, and I will look after myself. Thus watched and guarded each by himself, we will do our act, get a good fee, and come down safe and sound from the bamboo pole. That is the way to do it." Then the Lord said: "Just as the pupil said to the master: 'I will protect myself' - so should you practise the foundations of mindfulness which means at the same time: 'I will protect others.' By protecting oneself, one protects others. By protecting others, one protects oneself. And how does one, by protecting oneself, protect others? It is by the repeated and frequent practice of meditation. And how does one, by protecting others, protect oneself? It is by patience, forbearance, harmlessness, love and compassion."

Social Relationships

75.　　　Those families where mother and father are worshipped in the home are said to be like Brāhmā, like teachers of old; they are ranked with the gods of old. Truly worthy of offerings are those families where mother and father are worshipped in the home. "Brāhmā", "teachers of old", "gods of old", and "worthy of offerings" are terms for mother and father. And why? Because mother and father do much for children - they bring them up, nourish them and introduce them to the world.

76.　　　When a good man is reborn into a family, it is for the good, the welfare and the happiness of many - his parents, his wife and children, his servants and workers, his friends and companions and also for the good, the welfare and the happiness of recluses and Brāhmins.

77.　　　In five ways, a husband should minister to his wife. He should honour her, he should never disparage her, he should not be unfaithful to her, he should give her authority, and he should give her adornments. In five ways, a wife should reciprocate by ministering to her husband. She should organise her work properly, she should be kind to the servants, she should not be unfaithful to him, she should protect what he brings home, and she should be skilful and diligent in all she does.

78.   The householder Nakulapitā and his wife Nakulamātā came to see the Lord, and having sat down, Nakulapitā said: "Lord, since my wife was brought home to me when I was a mere boy, she being a mere girl, I have not been conscious of having transgressed against her even in thought, much less in body. Lord, we desire to behold each other, not just in this life, but in the next life also."

Nakulamātā then said: "Lord, since I was brought home to my husband's house when I was a mere girl, he being a mere boy, I have not been conscious of having transgressed against him even in thought, much less in body. Lord, we desire to behold each other, not just in this life, but in the next life also."

At this, the Lord said: "If both husband and wife desire to behold each other in both this life and the next life, and both are matched in faith, matched in virtue, matched in generosity and matched in wisdom, then they will behold each other in both this life and the next life also."

79.   One who could but does not
Support his mother and father
In their old age -

This is a cause of one's downfall.

80.   Wherever these five are found, whether in a king or a farmer, a general, a village headman, a guild master or the leaders of the clan, growth and not decline may be expected. What five?

Take the case of a clansman who has wealth acquired by work and effort, gathered by strength of arm and sweat of brow, and justly obtained by lawful means and who honours, reveres, venerates and respects his parents. They in turn regard him fondly with thoughts of love, and say: "Long life to you and may you be protected." Thus for one who regards his parents fondly, growth may be expected and not decline. The same is also true for his wife and children, servants and workfolk. The same obtains for those who work his fields, and his tenants, and also for the gods; the same applies to recluses and Brāhmins. When he regards them fondly, they will say: "Long life to you and may you be protected."

81.   Whatever families endure long, all of them do so because of four reasons, or because of several of them. What four? They recover what is lost, repair what is decayed, eat and drink in moderation, and they put in authority a man or woman of virtue.

82.   Monks! Brāhmins and householders are most helpful to you since they provide you with robe, bowl, lodging and seat, medicines and the necessities for sickness.

You also are most helpful to Brāhmins and householders, since you teach them the Dhamma that is lovely in the beginning, lovely in the middle and lovely at the end, both in letter and spirit. You proclaim to them the holy life in all its completeness and purity. Therefore, the holy life is lived in mutual dependence, for crossing the flood, for the overcoming of suffering.

83.　　　There are two people you can never repay. What two? Your father and your mother. Even if you were to carry them on your back and live a hundred years, supporting them, anointing them with medicines, bathing and massaging their limbs and wiping up their excrement after them, even this would not repay them. Even if you were to give them absolute rule over the whole world, this would not repay them. And why? Because parents do much for their children - they bring them up, nourish them, they introduce them to the world. But whoever encourages his unbelieving parents to believe, his immoral parents to be virtuous, his stingy parents to be generous, his foolish parents to be wise, such a one by so doing does repay, does more than repay his parents.

84.　　　In five ways, a child should minister to his mother and father. He should think: "Having been supported by them, I will support them in return. I will perform their duty for them. I will maintain the family traditions. I will be worthy of my heritage. After their death, I will distribute gifts on my parents' behalf."

In five ways, parents reciprocate by ministering to their children. They should restrain them from evil, encourage them to do good, teach them some craft, find them a suitable spouse, and in due time they should hand over their inheritance to them.

85.　　　In five ways, students should minister to their teachers, by rising to greet them, waiting on them, being attentive, serving them, and by mastering the skills they teach.

In five ways, teachers should reciprocate by ministering to their students. They should teach them carefully, make sure they understand what should be understood, give them a thorough grounding in all skills, recommend them to their friends and colleagues, and they should protect them in all directions.

86.　　　And how do disciples conduct themselves towards a teacher with love, not hostility? Concerning this, the compassionate teacher teaches the Dhamma to his disciples, seeking their welfare, out of compassion, saying: "This is for your welfare and happiness." His disciples listen to him, lend an ear, and prepare their minds for profound knowledge; they do not turn aside or move away from the teacher's instructions. Thus do disciples conduct themselves towards a teacher with love, not hostility. Therefore, conduct yourselves towards me with love, not hostility, and it will be for your welfare and happiness for a long time.

87.   A teacher should look upon his pupil as a son. A pupil should look upon his teacher as a father. Thus, these two, united by mutual reverence and deference and living in communion together will achieve increase, growth and progress in this Dhamma and discipline.

Love

88.   When one with a mind of love
Feels compassion for all the world,
Above, below and across,
Unlimited everywhere,

Filled with infinite kindness,
Complete and developed,
Any limited actions one may have done
Do not remain lingering in one's mind.

89.   I have heard this said: "Sublime is abiding in love," and the Lord is proof of this because he is seen to abide in love.

90.   Just as the radiance of all the stars is not worth one/ sixteenth part of the moon's radiance; just as in the last month of the rainy season, in autumn, when the sky is clear and free from clouds, the sun rises into the sky and drives away all darkness and shines, flashes and radiates; just as in the pre-dawn light, the healing star shines, flashes and radiates; so too, whatever good deeds one might do for the purpose of a good rebirth,

none of them are worth one/sixteenth part of that love which frees the mind. It is the love that frees the mind which shines, flashes and radiates forth, surpassing all those good deeds.

91.   Love is characterised as promoting the welfare of others. Its function is to desire welfare. It is manifested as the removal of annoyance. Its proximate cause is seeing the loveableness in beings. It succeeds when it makes ill-will subside, and it fails when it gives rise to selfish affection.

Compassion is characterised as promoting the removal of others' suffering. Its function is not bearing others' suffering. It is manifested as kindness. Its proximate cause is seeing helplessness in those overwhelmed by suffering. It succeeds when it makes cruelty subside, and it fails when it gives rise to sorrow.

Sympathetic joy is characterised as joy in the success of others. Its function is being free from envy. It is manifested as the elimination of aversion. Its proximate cause is seeing other beings' success. It succeeds when it makes aversion subside, and it fails when it gives rise to merriment.

Equanimity is characterised as promoting equipoise towards beings. Its function is to see the equality in beings. It is manifested as quieting like and dislike. Its proximate cause is seeing the ownership of deeds thus: "Beings are heirs to their deeds. Whose, if not theirs, is the choice by which they will become happy, or will be free from suffering, or will not fall away from the success they have reached?" It succeeds when it makes like and dislike subside, and it fails when it gives rise to the indifference of ignorance based on the household life.

92. When the Enlightened One or the Enlightened One's disciples live in the world, it is done for the good of the many, for the happiness of the many, out of compassion for the world - for the good, the welfare and the happiness of gods and men. And who is an Enlightened One? Concerning this, an Enlightened One arises in the world, a Noble One, a fully enlightened Buddha, of perfect knowledge and conduct, happily attained, a knower of the worlds, a guide unsurpassed of men to be trained, a teacher of gods and men, a Buddha, the Lord.
And who is an Enlightened One's disciple? He is one who teaches Dhamma that is lovely at the beginning, lovely in the middle and lovely at the end, both in the letter and in the spirit. He makes plain the holy life, entirely complete and purified. This is the Enlightened One and the Enlightened One's disciple, and when they live in the world, it is done for the good of the many, for the happiness of the many, out of compassion for the world, for the good, the welfare, the happiness of gods and men.

93. The noble quality of love should be thought about thus: "One concerned only with his own welfare, without concern for the welfare of others, cannot achieve success in this world or happiness in the next.

How then can one wishing to help all beings but not having love himself succeed in attaining Nirvāna? And if you wish to lead all beings to the supramundane state of Nirvāna, you should begin by wishing for their mundane welfare here and now." One should think: "I cannot provide for the welfare and happiness of others merely by wishing it. Let me make an effort to accomplish it." One should think: "Now I support them by promoting their welfare and happiness, and later they will be my companions in sharing the Dhamma." Then one should think: "Without these beings, I could not accumulate the requisites of enlightenment. Because they are the reason for practising and perfecting all the Buddha-qualities, these beings are for me the highest field of merit, the incomparable basis for planting wholesome roots, and thus the ultimate object of reverence." So, one should arouse an especially strong inclination towards promoting the welfare of all beings. And why should love be developed towards all beings? Because it is the foundation of compassion. For when one delights in providing for the welfare and happiness of other beings with an unbounded heart, the desire to remove their afflictions and suffering becomes strongly and firmly established. And compassion is the pre-eminent quality in Buddhahood, it is its basis, its foundation, its root, its head and its chief.

94.   When you speak to others, you might speak at the right time or at the wrong time, according to fact or

not, gently or harshly, about the goal or not, with a mind full of love or with a mind full of hatred. In this way, you should train yourself: "Our minds will not be perverted nor will we utter evil speech, but kindly and compassionately we will live with a mind full of love, without hatred. We will live having suffused ourselves with a mind full of love, and beginning with ourselves, we will live suffusing the whole world with a love that is far reaching, widespread, immeasurable, without enmity, without malevolence." This is how you should train yourself.

95.   If one were to give a gift of a hundred coins in the morning, again at noon and again in the evening, or instead, if one were to develop the mind of love in the morning, at noon and in the evening, although only for as long as it takes to pull a cow's udder, this would be by far the more beneficial of the two. Therefore, you should train yourself, thinking: "We will develop the liberation of the mind through love. We will practise it often. We will make it our vehicle and foundation. We will take our stand upon it, store it up and promote it."

96.   Eleven advantages are to be looked for in the freedom of mind through the practice of love, by making love grow, by making much of it, by making love a vehicle and basis, by persisting in it, by becoming familiar with it, and by establishing it well. What eleven? One sleeps happily and wakes happily, one has no bad dreams, one

is dear to both human and non-human beings, one is guarded by the gods; fire, poison and swords do not affect one, the mind concentrates quickly, the complexion is clean, one dies without bewilderment, and if one develops no further, one will reach at least to the Brāhmā world.

97.   If anyone abuses you to your face, strikes you with a fist, throws clods of earth at you, beats you with a stick or gives you a blow with a sword, you must put aside all worldly desires and considerations and train yourself like this: "My heart will be unwavering. No evil words shall I speak. I will live with compassion for the good of others, with a kindly heart, without resentment." Thus must you train yourself.

98.   As a mongoose approaches a snake to seize it only after having supplied his own body with medicine, so too, the meditator, the earnest student of meditation, on approaching this world abounding as it is in anger and malice, plagued by quarrels, strife, contention and hatred, must anoint his mind with the medicine of love.

99.   Even if low-down criminals should cut you limb from limb with a double-handled saw, if you filled your mind with hatred, you would not be practising my teachings.

100.   One should not blame another

Or despise anyone for any reason anywhere.
Do not wish pain upon another
Out of either anger or rivalry.

Just as a mother protects her only child
Even at the risk of her own life,
Even so, one cultivates unbounded love
Towards all beings in the world.

101.   Compassion is that which makes the heart of the good move at the pain of others. It crushes and destroys the pain of others; thus, it is called compassion. It is called compassion because it shelters and embraces the distressed.

102.   Whoever makes love grow boundless,
And sets his mind for seeing the end of birth,
His fetters are worn thin.

If he loves even a single being,
Good will follow.
But the Noble One
With compassionate heart for all mankind
Generates abounding good.

103.   If, for just as long as it takes to snap a finger, a monk thinks, develops and gives attention to the thought of love, then such a one is called a true monk. His meditation is not barren. He abides following the

Teacher's instructions. He is one who takes good advice and eats the country's alms-food to good purpose. What then could I say of one who makes much of such a thought?

104.   Conquer anger with love,
      Evil with good,
      Meanness with generosity,
      And lies with truth.

105.   There is one person who is born into the world for the welfare of the many, for the happiness of the many, out of compassion for the world, for the welfare and happiness of gods and man. Who is that person? It is the Enlightened One, the Noble One, the fully enlightened Buddha.

106.   "He abused me, he hit me,
      He oppressed me, he robbed me."
      Those who continue to hold such thoughts
      Never still their hatred.

      "He abused me, he hit me,
      He oppressed me, he robbed me."
      Those who do not continue to hold such thoughts
      Soon still their hatred.

      For in this world,
      Hatred is never appeased by more hatred;

It is love that conquers hatred.
This is an external law.

107.　　　And what is a monk's wealth? Concerning this, one abides with the mind filled with love, compassion, sympathetic joy and equanimity, suffusing the first, second, third and fourth quarters. One abides suffusing the whole world - upwards, downwards, across, everywhere - with a mind filled with love, compassion, sympathetic joy and equanimity; abundant, unbounded, without hatred or ill-will. This is a monk's wealth.

108.　　　Just as water cools both good and bad,
And washes away all impurity and dust,
In the same way you should develop thoughts of love
To friend and foe alike,
And having reached perfection in love,
You will attain enlightenment.

109.　　　An enlightened person is naturally endowed with a compassionate nature and disposition. He desires to alleviate the suffering that beings suffer, and is even willing to relinquish his own body or life to do so. Until he reaches his goal, he is willing to struggle and strive for a very long time on a course involving great hardship, without fear and without ever becoming disenchanted with all the suffering in the round of existence, all for the sake of the welfare of other beings.

Meditation and the Mind

110.   "What do you think about this?" said the Lord. "What is the purpose of a mirror?"

"It is for the purpose of reflection, sir," replied Rāhula.

"Even so, an action to be done by body, speech or mind should only be done after careful reflection."

111.   For one who is a learner and who has not yet come to the mastery of his mind, but who dwells aspiring for peace from bonds, making it a matter concerning himself, I know of no other thing so helpful as giving close attention to his mind.

112.   Develop the meditation that is mindfulness of in-and-out breathing. Mindfulness of in-and-out breathing is of great fruit, of great advantage. And how is mindfulness of in-and-out breathing developed, how is it made much of, how is it of great fruit, great advantage? Concerning this, one goes to the forest, to the root of a tree or to an empty place, sits down cross-legged with the back straight, establishing mindfulness

in front of him. Mindfully one breathes in, mindfully one breathes out. Breathing in a long breath one knows: "I am breathing in a long breath;" breathing out a long breath one knows: "I am breathing out a long breath." Breathing in a short breath one knows: "I am breathing in a short breath;" breathing out a short breath one knows: "I am breathing out a short breath." One trains oneself, thinking: "Breathing in I shall experience the whole body." One trains oneself, thinking: "Breathing out I shall experience the whole body." One trains oneself, thinking: "Breathing in I will tranquillise bodily activities." One trains oneself, thinking: "Breathing out I will tranquillise bodily activities."

113. Wonderful it is to tame the mind;
   Difficult to tame, restless
   And seizing whatever it desires.
   A tamed mind brings happiness.

114. There are these five debasements of gold, which make it not pliable, workable or glistening, but brittle and incapable of perfect workmanship. What five? Iron, copper, tin, lead and silver. But when gold is free from these five debasements it is pliable, workable and glistening, not brittle and capable of perfect workmanship. Then whatever sort of ornament one wants, be it a signet ring, earring, necklace or a gold chain, it can be used for that.

  In the same way, there are these five debasements of

the mind because of which the mind is not pliable, workable, or glistening, but is brittle and badly composed for the destruction of the defilements. What five? Sense desire, ill-will, sloth, worry and doubt. But when the mind is free from these five debasements, it is pliable, workable, glistening, not brittle but well composed for the destruction of the defilements. Then one can direct the mind to the realisation by psychic knowledge of whatever can be realised by psychic knowledge and can see it directly, whatever its range might be.

115.   This intent concentration on in-and-out breathing, if cultivated and developed, is something peaceful and excellent, something perfect in itself and a pleasant way of living also. Not only that, it dispels evil unskilled thoughts that have arisen and makes them vanish in a moment. It is just as when, in the last month of the hot season, the dust and dirt fly up and suddenly a great rain falls upon them and makes them settle in a moment.

116.   One who is intent on developing higher thought should attend to five things from time to time. What five?
    If, while attending to something, evil unskilful thoughts associated with greed, hatred and delusion should arise, then one should attend instead to something that is skilful. Then these evil unskilful

thoughts will subside and the mind will be steady, calmed, one-pointed and concentrated. It is just as if a carpenter or his apprentice might knock out, drive out, or draw out a large peg with a small one.

If, while attending to something that is skilled, evil unskilful thoughts associated with greed, hatred and delusion still arise, then one should ponder the disadvantages of those thoughts, thinking: "Truly, these thoughts are unskilful, blameworthy and conducive to suffering." Then those evil unskilful thoughts will subside and the mind will be steady, calm, one-pointed and concentrated. It is just as if a well-dressed young man or woman, on having the carcass of a snake, a dog or a human being hung around his or her neck would be repelled, ashamed and disgusted.

If, however, while pondering the disadvantages of these thoughts, evil unskilful thoughts associated with greed, hatred and delusion still arise, then one should forget about them, pay them no attention. Then those evil unskilful thoughts will subside and the mind will be steady, calm, one-pointed and concentrated. It is just as if a man with sight might shut his eyes or turn away in order to avoid seeing something.

But if, while trying to forget about and paying no attention to those thoughts, evil unskilful thoughts associated with greed, hatred and delusion still arise, then one should allow them to settle. Then those evil unskilful thoughts will subside and the mind will be steady, calm, one-pointed and concentrated. It is just as if a man, finding no reason for running, walks; then finding no reason for walking, stands; then finding no reason for standing, sits down; then finding no reason for sitting, lies down. Thus he goes from a strenuous posture to a more relaxed one.

But if, while allowing those thoughts to settle, evil unskilful thoughts associated with greed, hatred and delusion still arise, then, with teeth clenched and tongue pressed against the palate one should restrain, subdue and suppress the mind with the mind. Then those evil unskilful thoughts will subside and the mind will be steady, calm, one-pointed and concentrated. It is just as if a strong man should hold down a weaker one by seizing his head and shoulders.

One who does these things is called a master of the pathways of thought. The thought he wants to think, he thinks, the thought he does not want to think, he does not think. He has cut off craving, removed the fetters, mastered pride and put an end to suffering.

117. One remembers and turns over in the mind thoughts about things based on desire in the past, present and future. As one does so, desire is generated, and being desirous one is fettered by those things. And when a mind is full of lust that is what I call a fetter.

118. Giving up worldly desires, one dwells with a mind free from worldly desires and is purified. Giving up ill-will and hatred, one dwells with a mind filled with compassion and love for the welfare of all beings, and purifies the mind of ill-will and hatred. Giving up sloth

and laziness, one perceives the light, and mindful and clearly comprehending, one purifies the mind of sloth and laziness. Giving up restlessness and worry and remaining inwardly calm, one purifies the mind of restlessness and worry. Giving up doubt, one crosses over doubt, and without uncertainty as to what is skilful, one purifies the mind of doubt.

Just as a man who had borrowed money to develop his business, and whose business has prospered, might repay the money and have enough left over to support a wife, and would think: "Before I was in debt, but now I am free from debt," and would be glad and happy because of that;

Just as a man who was sick and suffering, without appetite and weak, might in time regain his health, appetite and strength, and would think: "Before I was sick, but now I am healthy," and would be glad and happy because of that;

Just as a man who was imprisoned might, after a time, be freed without any confiscation of his property, and would think: "Before I was imprisoned, but now I am free," and would be glad and happy because of that;

Just as a man who was enslaved, not his own master, controlled by another and unable to do as he desired, and who in time might be emancipated, would think: "I was a slave, but now I am emancipated," and would be glad and happy because of that;

Just as a traveller carrying goods and wealth who found himself in a wilderness with little food and much danger, and after a time, might arrive safe and sound at the edge of a village, and would think: "Before I was in danger, but now I am safe," and would be glad and happy because of that;

In the same way, as long as the five hindrances are not given up, one feels indebted, sick, imprisoned, enslaved and lost in the wilderness. But when the five hindrances are given up, one feels free from debt, healthy, free, emancipated and safe. And when one knows that these five hindrances are given up, gladness arises, from gladness comes joy, because of joy the body is tranquil, with a tranquil body one is happy, and the mind of one who is happy is concentrated.

119.   Whatever one thinks about and ponders over often, one's mind gets a leaning in that way.

120.   That which is called thought, mind or consciousness arises and disappears continuously both day and night. Just as a monkey swinging through the trees grabs one branch, letting it go only to grab another, so too that which is called thought, mind or consciousness arises and disappears continuously both day and night.

121.   I know not of any other single thing so unworkable as the undeveloped mind. Indeed, the undeveloped mind is an unworkable thing. I know not of any other single thing so workable as the developed mind. Indeed, the developed mind is a workable thing.

122.   Whatever has had to be done by a teacher out of compassion, for the welfare of his disciples, I have done for you. Here are the roots of the trees, here are the empty places. Meditate, do not be slothful, do not be remorseful later. These are my instructions to you.

123.   The mind is luminous, but it is stained by defilements that come from without. Ordinary folk do not realise this, so they do not cultivate the mind. The mind is luminous, but it can be cleansed of defilements that come from without. This the noble disciples understand, so they do cultivate the mind.

124.   Whatever harm an enemy can do to an enemy,
        Or a hater to a hater,
        An ill-directed mind
        Causes oneself even greater harm.

        No mother or father
        Or any other kin
        Can do greater good for oneself
        Than a well-directed mind.

Sickness and Health

125.　　There are these three types of sick persons to be found in the world. What three?

There is the sick person who, whether he obtains the proper diet, proper medicines, proper nursing or not, will not recover from his illness.

Again, there is the sick person who, whether he obtains the proper diet, the proper medicines, the proper nursing or not, will recover from his illness anyway.

And again, there is the sick person who will recover from his illness only if he gets the proper diet, medicines and nursing.

It is for this last type that proper diet, medicine and nursing should be prescribed, but the others should be looked after also.

Now, there are three types of persons in the world who can be compared to the three types of sick persons. What three?

There is the person who, whether he gets a chance of seeing the Enlightened One and learning the Dhamma and discipline or not, will not enter the perfection of things that are skilful.

Again, there is the person who, whether he gets a chance of seeing the Enlightened One and learning the

Dhamma and discipline or not, will enter the perfection of things that are skilful.

And again, there is the person who will enter into the perfection of things that are skilful only if he gets a chance of seeing the Enlightened One and learning the Dhamma and discipline.

It is on account of this last person that the Dhamma is proclaimed, but it should be taught to the others also.

126.   Good health is the highest gain,
         And contentment is the greatest wealth.
         Trust is the best of kinsmen,
         And Nirvāna is the highest happiness.

127.   Possessed of five qualities, a sick man is of much help to himself? What five? He knows what medicine is good for him, he knows the right measure in his treatment, he takes the medicine, he describes his illness to the one who nurses him out of kindness, saying: "In going, it goes like this; in coming, it comes like this; while there, it is like this," and he is one who endures the various pains of the sickness.

128.   Possessing five qualities, one who nurses the sick is fit to nurse the sick. What five? He can prepare the medicine; he knows what is good and what is not - what is good he offers, and what is not he does not; he nurses

the sick out of love, not out of hope for gain; he is unmoved by excrement, urine, vomit and spittle; and, from time to time he can instruct, inspire, gladden and satisfy the sick with talk on Dhamma.

129. The Buddha is like a skilled physician in that he is able to heal the sickness of the defilements. The Dhamma is like a rightly applied medicine, and those in the Sangha, with their defilements cured, are like people restored to health by that medicine.

130.
If a man suffering from a disease
Does not seek treatment
Even when there is a physician at hand,
It is not the fault of the physician.

In the same way, if one is oppressed
And tormented by the disease of the defilements
But does not seek help from the Teacher,
That is not the Teacher's fault.

References

1. Sāmyutta Nikāya, V: 457.
2. Dhammapada, 53.
3. Samyutta Nikāya, II: 263.
4. Anguttara Nikāya, V: 120.
5. Sutta Nipāta, 574-581.
6. Anguttara Nikāya, III: 71.
7. Samyutta Nikāya, V: 369.
8. Dhammapada, 6.
9. Dhammapada Atthakatā, 273.
10. Jātaka Nīdānakathā, 120-122.
11. Anguttara Nikāya, III: 243.
12. Dīgha Nikāya, I: 64.
13. Anguttara Nikāya, II: 78.
14. Sutta Nipāta, 450-454.
15. Majjhima Nikāya, I: 500.
16. Anguttara Nikāya, II: 172.
17. Anguttara Nikāya, II: 97.
18. Dīgha Nikāya, I: 3.
19. Majjhima Nikāya, I: 161.
20. Sutta Nipāta, 720-721.
21. Anguttara Nikāya, I: 197.
22. Dhammapada, 227-229.
23. Itivuttaka, 18.

24.   Anguttara Nikāya, III: 38.
25   Dhammapada, 354.
26.   Anguttara Nikāya, I: 161.
27.   Anguttara Nikāya, III: 172.
28.   Anguttara Nikāya, III: 41.
29.   Anguttara Nikāya, I: 150.
30.   Dīgha Nikāya, III: 107.
31.   Dhammapada, 304.
32.   Samyutta Nikāya, V: 354.
33.   Dhammapada, 121-122.
34.   Anguttara Nikāya, V: 266.
35.   Anguttara Nikāya, I: 294.
36.   Theragātha, 608-609; 612-613.
37.   Anguttara Nikāya, I: 101.
38.   Dhammapada, 16; 18.
39.   Milindapañha, 195.
40   Milindapañha, 84.
41.   Anguttara Nikāya, I: 58.
42.   Anguttara Nikāya, V: 2.
43.   Dhammapada, 110.
44.   Itivuttaka, 15.
45.   Udana, 87.
46.   Dīgha Nikāya, I: 84.
47.   Anguttara Nikāya, III: 259.
48.   Anguttara Nikāya, I: 15.
49.   Anguttara Nikāya, IV: 6.
50.   Anguttara Nikāya, IV: 281.
51.   Anguttara Nikāya, III: 207.
52.   Dīgha Nikāya, III: 184.
53.   Anguttara Nikāya, IV: 269.
54.   Dīgha Nikāya, III: 192.

55. Anguttara Nikāya, IV: 30.
56. Theragātha, 1018-1019.
57. Dhammapada, 76-77.
58. Samyutta Nikāya, I: 71.
59. Dīgha Nikāya, III: 186.
60. Dhammasangani, 1328.
61. Samyutta Nikāya, V: 2.
62. Itivuttaka, 68.
63. Anguttara Nikāya, V: 79.
64. Anguttara Nikāya, II: 94.
65. Anguttara Nikāya, IV: 219.
66. Dhammapada, 50; 253; 159; 379.
67. Anguttara Nikāya, V: 91.
68. Anguttara Nikāya, V: 159.
69. Anguttara Nikāya, I: 9.
70. Majjhima Nikāya, I: 45.
71. Dhammapada, 129.
72. Majjhima Nikāya, I: 97.
73. Milindapañha, 410.
74. Samyutta Nikāya, V: 168.
75. Anguttara Nikāya, II: 69.
76. Anguttara Nikāya, III: 46.
77. Dīgha Nikāya, III: 190.
78. Anguttara Nikāya, II: 59.
79. Sutta Nipāta, 98.
80. Anguttara Nikāya, III: 76.
81. Anguttara Nikāya, II: 249.
82. Itivuttaka, 111.
83. Anguttara Nikāya, I: 61.
84. Dīgha Nikāya, III: 189.
85. Dīgha Nikāya, III: 189.

86. Majjhima Nikāya, III: 117-118.
87. Vinaya, IV: 45.
88. Jātaka, 37-38.
89. Majjhima Nikāya, I: 369.
90. Itivuttaka, 20.
91. Visuddhimagga, 318.
92. Anguttara Nikāya, II: 146.
93. Cariyāpitaka Atthakatā, 292.
94. Majjhima Nikāya, I: 126.
95. Samyutta Nikāya, II: 264.
96. Anguttara Nikāya, V: 342.
97. Majjhima Nikāya, I: 124.
98. Milindapañha, 394.
99. Majjhima Nikāya, I: 129.
100. Sutta Nipāta, 149-150.
101. Dhammapada Atthakatā, 193.
102. Anguttara Nikāya, IV: 151.
103. Anguttara Nikāya, I: 10.
104. Dhammapada, 223.
105. Anguttara Nikāya, I: 21.
106. Dhammapada, 3-5.
107. Dīgha Nikāya, III: 78.
108. Jātaka Nādanakath , 168-169.
109. Cariyāpitaka Atthakatā, 278.
110. Majjhima Nikāya, I: 415.
111. Itivuttaka, 9.
112. Majjhima Nikāya, I: 425.
113. Dhammapada, 35.
114. Anguttara Nikāya, III: 15.
115. Samyutta Nikāya, V: 321.
116. Majjhima Nikāya, I: 119.

117. Anguttara Nikāya, I: 263.
118. Dīgha Nikāya, I: 72.
119. Majjhima Nikāya, I: 115.
120. Samyutta Nikāya, II: 93.
121. Anguttara Nikāya, I: 4.
122. Majjhima Nikāya, I: 46.
123. Anguttara Nikāya, I: 10.
124. Dhammapada, 42-43.
125. Anguttara Nikāya, I: 121.
126. Dhammapada, 227.
127. Anguttara Nikāya, III: 143.
128. Anguttara Nikāya, III: 144.
129. Paramatthajotikā, 21.
130. Jātaka Nīdanakathā, 28-29.